CW00645895

NEW ZEALAND

NEW ZEALAND

A PHOTOGRAPHIC JOURNEY

TODD & SARAH SISSON

New Zealand
FINE TOURING GROUP

With Compliments
www.newzealandfinetouring.co.nz

First published in 2015 by Potton & Burton

Potton & Burton
98 Vickerman Street, PO Box 5128, Nelson, New Zealand
pottonandburton.co.nz

© Todd & Sarah Sisson

ISBN 978 1 927213 69 8

Printed in China by Midas Printing International Ltd

This book is copyright. Apart from any fair dealing for the purposes
of private study, research, criticism or review, as permitted under the
Copyright Act, no part may be reproduced by any process without
the permission of the publishers.

CONTENTS

INTRODUCTION

In the early phases of this book project we, along with our publisher Robbie Burton, resolved to compile a portfolio of images celebrating New Zealand's accessible landscapes – the hundreds of incredible scenic locations that most travellers can reach by vehicle or with a little moderate walking. This editorial decision was made very much in response to the everyday realities that have framed our photography careers – namely the demands of family life.

The discipline of landscape photography, with its early mornings, late nights, extensive travel and long periods of waiting, waiting and yet more waiting is often the domain of lone-wolf singletons and childless couples. Our decision to pursue a career in landscape photography was made while we were firmly ensconced in the childless couple camp, having been informed by several specialists that we were incapable of conceiving children.

Armed with the devil-may-care ethos of those who know they will never have to purchase diapers or finance kids through university, we proceeded to wind down our successful commercial photography studio, purchase a two-berth caravan and book tickets overseas to start building an image library. Two months later we were pregnant with our first son, Jack; his little sister Indi arrived on the scene 17 months later ...

The whole idea behind burning bridges is to make retreat impossible, and so it was for us, as we had little option but to continue on with our plans (or get real jobs). But the logistical difficulties of photographing nature with two busy infants are 'uniquely intense'. Consequently, we have yet to embark upon multi-week treks into New Zealand's remote wilderness areas, but this has not proven to be a problem for us whatsoever.

Proofing the manuscript for this book provided a poignant reminder of just how freakishly beautiful this small land really is – something that is easily overlooked after years of travelling and photographing one's home country. But New Zealand's truly unique attribute is just how easy it is for everyday people to experience its outstanding natural features. We have travelled other countries with fiords, glaciers, geysers, alps and beautiful lakes but these natural features always seem to be separated by huge distances with few points of interest in between. Not so in

Aotearoa, where one interesting landscape usually segues to the next within a hundred kilometres or so.

Of course, we the public get to share in much of New Zealand's natural beauty by virtue of the actions of those far-sighted individuals, groups and politicians who saw-fit to vest so many of our significant landscapes to the public domain. Without these actions it is quite possible to envisage internationally renowned locations like Milford Sound under corporate ownership or serving as a billionaire's private playground.

That is why we are so lucky to live in this country. A career such as ours, which lets us combine our work and family time while witnessing a diverse array of natural landscapes, would simply not be viable in most countries.

We hope that this book will be received as a keepsake or travel companion for like-minded individuals who share our deep appreciation of this special country. It must be said that many of the images in this book document brief moments when weather, light and photographic vision unite to produce a unique representation of a location. Many of these images were made after excruciatingly early starts and, consequently, most

visitors will never witness the landscape in this way – we only hope that our photographic efforts help to enhance your appreciation of New Zealand's exquisite natural realm.

– Todd and Sarah Sisson

QUEENSTOWN AND WANAKA

Often referred to collectively as the Southern Lakes, Queenstown and Wanaka possess some of New Zealand's best-known landscape scenery. The view from Queenstown's lakeshore to the Remarkables mountain range undoubtedly ranks as one of New Zealand's most identifiable scenes. Journey over the switchbacks of the Crown Range highway and yet more alpine majesty reveals itself on the shores of Lake Wanaka and Lake Hawea. Beautiful year-round, Wanaka is simply sublime in late autumn when the poplar and willow trees trim the landscape in gold.

Our home in Central Otago is situated less than an hour's drive from either Queenstown or Wanaka and we visit both towns regularly. One would expect the sense of awe to subside over the years, but the visual impact of the myriad views contained within this compact area never seems to dull with familiarity.

Given the abundance of world-class scenery shoehorned into the Southern Lakes area, it would be reasonable to expect that great landscape images could be achievable by simply turning up and pointing a camera in any given direction during daylight hours. It is no small irony then that both Queenstown and Wanaka are deceptively difficult locations to photograph well.

The reason for this paradox is geography. Compelling landscape images are created when beautiful light casts itself upon beautiful landforms. The richest, most ethereal light occurs during a narrow window early in the morning and late in the evening. For much of the year, particularly in Queenstown, the best light is blocked at sunrise and sunset by the very things that we are endeavouring to capture – the tall mountains that form the backbone of the landscape.

The images in this chapter have been collected over the past decade. Many represent those fleeting moments when weather, location and light intersect to create an image that was equal to or greater than the one formed by our 'minds eye'. A rare thing indeed.

'The Lady of the Lake', TSS *Earnslaw* steams toward Queenstown Harbour, with Cecil Peak in the background. ss

Mid-summer offers the best chance for witnessing sunset colour in Queenstown. On this occasion, a clearing storm captured the evening light over Lake Wanaka. TS OPPOSITE Queenstown and the Remarkables at sunset, as viewed from Bob's Peak. SS

Autumn snow on the Richardson Mountains, Skippers Canyon, Queenstown. TS
OPPOSITE Alpine tussocks on the Crown Range, Queenstown. SS
OVERLEAF First light on Mt Earnslaw, from Bennett's Bluff on the Queenstown–Glenorchy road. TS

The Wakatipu Basin from Coronet Peak. SS
OPPOSITE Near Chard Farm winery, Gibbston Valley, Queenstown. TS

Early snow on the Remarkables, Queenstown. ss

A pristine autumn afternoon at Lake Hayes, with Cecil Peak in the distance. ss

Double Cone at sunset, the Remarkables, Queenstown. TS
OPPOSITE Cecil Peak on a winter's evening, from Coronet Peak. TS

Lake Wakatipu from the Remarkables skifield. TS
OPPOSITE Crown Terrace, Queenstown, on a late summer evening. TS
OVERLEAF Dramatic spot-lighting near Minaret Bay, Lake Wanaka. SS

Autumnal landscape, Cardrona Valley. SS
OPPOSITE Poplars in clearing dawn mist, near Wanaka. TS
OVERLEAF Morning reflections in Lake Wanaka. SS

Sunrise on the Lake Wanaka foreshore. ss
OPPOSITE Moonrise over Lake Hawea. ss
OVERLEAF Farmland along the Cardrona Valley highway. ss

CENTRAL OTAGO

Tucked away in the core of the lower South Island, 'Central', as it is commonly known, stands apart from its evergreen neighbours as a semi-arid and sparsely populated enclave. Central's landscape is buttressed on all sides by mountains that wring most storms dry long before they reach the interior. This results in clear skies, hot, dry summers and crisp, cold winter days.

The weather expresses itself on a landscape of odd contrasts rarely seen elsewhere in New Zealand. Jagged rock outcrops jut starkly from softly rolling hillsides; lakes, ponds and rivers abound in the parched golden brown landscape; while tall mountains often appear diminutive due to their rounded and unimposing forms.

Then there is the light. Clear, unpolluted skies provide little resistance to the southern sun, producing a sharp, often harsh light that plays out wonderfully on this landscape – revealing and accentuating the gentle drapes and folds of the Central Otago landscape.

These juxtapositions, combined with the low-key lifestyle, drew us to Central Otago many years ago and continue to captivate us with under-stated natural beauty and boundless photographic opportunities. It is a joy to share this often-over-looked corner of the country with you.

Stockyards and the Hawkdun Range. ss

The last of the day's light at the Blue Lake, St Bathans. ss
OPPOSITE Early morning light at Butchers Dam, near our home in Alexandra. TS
OVERLEAF Rocky tors along the Old Dunstan Road, east of Poolburn Reservoir. TS

An early autumn morning on Lake Dunstan. TS
opposite Ruins and rolling farmland near Shingle Creek, Roxburgh Gorge. TS

Atop the Raggedy Range, near Omakau. TS

Merino sheep grazing near Duffers Saddle, with Lake Dunstan and Cromwell in the distance. ss
OVERLEAF The Hawkdun Range reflected in Falls Dam, near St Bathans. ss

Evening light on Lindis Pass hills. ss
OPPOSITE Spaniard, or speargrasses, at Duffers Saddle on the Nevis Valley Road. TS

A mid-winter morning at Lowburn. ss

Evening light on the Hawkdun Range. TS

COASTAL OTAGO AND SOUTHLAND

In the late 1990s we drove through the Catlins to the south coast for the first time. At some point, south of Balclutha, it genuinely seemed as if we had accidentally passed through a space–time portal and emerged on New Zealand's forgotten coast.

In many ways we had. The remote and sparsely populated southern reaches of the country commanded very little mindshare among New Zealanders. At the time, it is likely that most Aucklanders believed the word 'Catlins' referred to an American soul-food dish featuring polecat entrails and corn grits. On reflection, that probably still holds true ...

But an interesting trend was evident on that trip. New Zealanders may have lost this corner of the country but foreign travellers had found it and loved what it had to offer – rugged coastline, wild weather, rare wildlife and isolated beaches devoid of human crowds. A steady trickle of dilapidated camper vans full of (mainly) European tourists were traversing the southeast corner of our country and taking in all that it offered!

A change of mindset rapidly ensued in the early 2000s – Dunedin discovered the Otago Peninsula on its doorstep, the Catlins highway was steadily upgraded and Invercargill imported a semi-exiled Auckland politician as its mayor and cheerleader-in-chief. The Deep South was suddenly back on the map and that trickle of camper vans is a torrent during the summer months today.

Photographically, Coastal Otago and Southland are scattered
with a number of gem locations, most of which are found where the land yields to the sea. Having lived in Dunedin for nine years, we feel qualified to state that photographing this part of the country is no easy task – thanks to the famously dismal weather that haunts the area.
The secret to photographing this neck of the woods is to muster patience (easy to write, hard to do) and work with the conditions to capitalise on the climatic drama that is relentlessly hurled forth by the roaring forties.

Dawn at Moeraki Beach. TS

A yellow-eyed penguin returns home under dramatic clouds, Moeraki Peninsula. TS
OPPOSITE Portobello village and Harbour Cone, Otago Peninsula, Dunedin. TS
OVERLEAF Sunrise over the Moeraki boulders, Moeraki Beach. TS

Taiaroa Head, at the mouth of Otago Harbour. ss

Sunrise over Otago Peninsula from Peggy's Hill. TS

Southerly swells batter the cliffs at Tunnel Beach, Dunedin. TS

OPPOSITE Sunrise at Tunnel Beach, Dunedin. SS

Farmland on Sandymount, Otago. TS
OPPOSITE Sunrise over Nugget Point, Catlins coast. SS

Lower McLean Falls, Catlins Coastal Rainforest Park. ss
OPPOSITE Tautuku River, Catlins Coastal Rainforest Park. TS
OVERLEAF Late summer near Orepuki, Southland. ss

Purakaunui Bay, Catlins coast. ss
OPPOSITE Stooked oats, Lochiel, Southland. ss

FIORDLAND

Fiordland National Park presides over a huge tract of mountainous wilderness in the southwestern corner of the South Island. Fiordland's grandeur is the byproduct of two irresistible natural forces – glaciation and plate tectonics. The immense glaciers of ice ages past cleaved Fiordland's deep U-shaped fiords and valleys from granite mountains ejected from the Tasman Sea by the colliding Australian and Pacific plates – a process that continues to this day.

Fiordland is a fortress formed by extreme geography, geology and weather. The region is further bolstered by a series of moat-like lakes to the east and the Tasman Sea to the west. It seems entirely plausible that you could spend the best part of a lifetime exploring Fiordland without ever experiencing its entirety. After all, this country managed to hide a remnant population of takahe, a bird species believed extinct for nearly fifty years.

In human terms, much of Fiordland is extremely difficult to access and rarely visited, other than by hardcore outdoor enthusiasts and hunters – many of whom access remote areas via helicopter or boat. The exceptions to this rule are Milford and Doubtful sounds, which can be reached by motor transport, thus eliminating the need to sleep under a tarpaulin and subsist on oatmeal during a week-long bush trek.

We have visited these two corners of Fiordland many times and the thrill of entering this natural wonderland never diminishes. Photographically, Milford Sound is in a class of its own, thanks to the sculpted form of Mitre Peak, which is uncannily situated within the fiord. However, our favourite part of a Milford visit is always the journey along the Milford road. There is almost a tempo to the way in which the scenery is distributed along its length – the grandeur seems to escalate around each major corner.

Doubtful Sound offers a very different photographic experience as it lacks a visual centrepiece comparable to Mitre Peak. It does, however, possess a different form of visual beauty – still stunningly spectacular but perhaps more subtle. Critically, Doubtful Sound receives far fewer visitors than Milford, meaning it is possible to experience moments of natural solitude – representative of the great tracts of Fiordland wilderness that many of us will never witness.

Evening light at Milford Sound. TS

Late afternoon at Milford Sound. ss

A tourist boat returns to Milford Sound harbour on a glorious afternoon. The mist in the middle ground of this scene is actually spray from the thundering Bowen Falls. ss

OVERLEAF The Milford Sound road winds down the Cleddau Valley under a clearing sky. ss

Early morning at Lake Gunn near the Divide, on the Milford road. ss

A perfect morning reflection at Milford Sound. TS

Overlooking Doubtful Sound from Wilmot Pass. TS
OPPOSITE First light on Mitre Peak, Milford Sound. SS

Sculpted boulders in the Gulliver River. SS
OPPOSITE Doubtful Sound, viewed from Real Journey's excursion launch, *Patea Explorer*. TS

Mt Christina and the Key Summit tarns at sunrise. TS
OPPOSITE Evening light on the Ailsa Mountains, from Key Summit. TS

THE WEST COAST

Referred to simply as 'the Coast' by most South Islanders, the West Coast is one of New Zealand's most unpopulated, remote and beautiful regions. The West Coast that most visitors experience is a narrow ribbon of land that wends between the Tasman Sea and a complex series of mountain ranges to the east.

The Coast's geography, and the resulting vistas, are largely defined by this tension between mountains, ocean and the extremely wet weather that eventuates when water-laden Tasman weather systems meet precipitous mountain ranges. The further south one ventures, the more dramatic the relationship between mountains and sea becomes, most notably near Fox Glacier where New Zealand's tallest peak, Aoraki/Mt Cook, stands 3750 metres above the coast at Gillespies Beach – less than 30 kilometres away.

North of Hokitika, the Alpine Fault's tectonic conveyor belt veers eastward toward Blenheim, carrying the torn and serrated peaks of the Southern Alps away from the coast. Ironically, this only makes the Coast more inaccessible, as the alps yield to a expansive jumble of low mountains clad in impenetrable native bush. This land was unforgiving to early European settlers, the deprivations of Thomas Brunner's 550-day survey mission from Nelson to Bruce Bay marking it as one of the colonial era's most epic expeditions.

From a photographic perspective, the Coast is our favourite New Zealand region – the reason for this being slightly oddball. Obviously, the spectacular landforms, raging rivers and dewy coastal light make the Coast a photographer's dream destination, but the same could be said for much of the South Island. The reason we love photographing the Coast is that it is always challenging – from the long travel distances on narrow, twisting roads to the mercurial weather patterns and savage sandflies, the Coast never makes things easy. In this day and age that makes for a wonderful place to visit!

The stunning morning view of Mt Tasman and Aoraki/Mt Cook from Lake Matheson. TS

Looking toward the Haast Range from the Arawhata River bridge, Jackson Bay. ss
OPPOSITE The Blue Pools, Haast Pass. ss

The upper reaches of the Makarora River from Cameron's Flat. TS
OPPOSITE Rimu forest meets the sea at Bruce Bay. SS

Sunset on the Southern Alps from Lake Matheson. TS
OPPOSITE Native trees silhouetted at sunset, Fox River flats. TS

ABOVE AND OPPOSITE Morning mist clears over the Fox River flats. SS

Just on sunset, a storm brews to the north of Punakaiki. TS

Water spouts through a blowhole at Dolomite Point, Punakaiki. TS
OVERLEAF Looking south across the Karamea River estuary. SS

Limestone patterns, Moria Gate Arch, Oparara Basin, Kahurangi National Park. SS
OPPOSITE Moria Gate Arch, Oparara Basin, Kahurangi National Park. TS

Tree ferns, near Karamea. ss
OPPOSITE Forest track, Karamea. TS

The Kohaihai River meets the Tasman Sea, Karamea. TS
OPPOSITE Coastal rainbow near Kohaihai Bluff, Karamea. SS

AORAKI/MT COOK
AND THE MACKENZIE COUNTRY

At Lindis Pass, State Highway 8 crosses north from Central Otago into the Mackenzie Basin, also known as the Mackenzie Country. This landscape shares much in common with Central Otago – it too is 'big sky country', an arid rain-shadow area of vast golden-brown plains.

But the Mackenzie Country's landscape is tattooed with a network of aqua blue canals and lakes, almost all of which are components of the massive Upper Waitaki hydroelectricity scheme. Where the water runs, life abounds, and during the warmer months swathes of exotic willow trees and Russell lupins bring lush colour to the Mackenzie.

Yet the greatest impression is made by the Mackenzie's backdrop – the Southern Alps. From the flat lands the Alps abruptly rise to reach their zenith on the high peak of Aoraki/Mt Cook, 3750 metres above sea level.

Aoraki/Mt Cook is somewhat of a 'free lunch' for landscape photographers. New Zealand's tallest peak could easily be have been robbed of its scale by surrounding peaks or located in a remote glacial valley and best viewed from an aircraft like spectacular Mt Aspiring to the south. Instead, Aoraki/Mt Cook's eastern faces stand completely unimpeded by lesser mountains, with its foreground framed from State Highway 8 by the icy blue glacial waters of Lake Pukaki.

The views and sense of scale only improve as you draw closer to the massif, the vista from the Hermitage Hotel being a truly world-class view. A walk up the Hooker River valley ends with Aoraki/Mt Cook standing sentinel over the Hooker Glacier terminal lake. This high alpine walk seems mildly adventurous until you witness tourists in full Gucci outfits replete with heels and gilt-edged handbags happily making their way uphill – there truly are few excuses for not exploring the beautiful alpine landscape on a visit to Mount Cook village!

Aoraki/Mt Cook at sunset. TS

Early morning in the Hooker Valley. TS
OPPOSITE Aoraki/Mt Cook and the Mount Cook Range from Hooker Lake. SS

Aoraki/Mt Cook from the eastern shores of Lake Pukaki. TS
OPPOSITE State Highway 80 at Peter's Lookout. SS

Clearing fog, Hooker Valley. TS

Mirror reflections, Hooker Lake. SS

Aoraki/Mt Cook from the shores of Lake Pukaki. TS
OPPOSITE Evening tranquility alongside the Tekapo–Pukaki canal. SS
OVERLEAF Sunrise on the Hall Range, Lake Tekapo. TS

Dawn pastels, Ahuriri River near Omarama. TS
OPPOSITE Russell lupins in flower, Lake Tekapo. SS

Russell lupins and the clay cliffs, Omarama. TS
OPPOSITE An autumn evening at Church of the Good Shepherd, Lake Tekapo. SS
OVERLEAF The holiday settlement at Lake Alexandrina, near Lake Tekapo. TS

CANTERBURY AND THE TOP OF THE SOUTH

The Canterbury region occupies a large portion of the South Island's eastern seaboard, stretching from the Waitaki River in the south to well north of Kaikoura township. Much of Canterbury's landscape is given over to the vast agrarian plains that span much of the region's 350-kilometre length.

Vast tracts of human-modified land tend to make for slim photographic pickings and our instincts have always been to head west where the plains meet the squat and rounded eastern flanks of the Southern Alps or northward to the rugged Kaikoura coastline where the Seaward Kaikoura mountains preside over a tract of Pacific Ocean that is teaming with wildlife.

Where Canterbury ends, the area often referred to as the Top of the South begins. The flat lands of the plains gradually transition into a tangle of foothills that make this part of the country a relatively demanding place to access. Todd's home town of Nelson and further afield in Golden Bay are places that you very much have to get 'into' and 'out of', being boxed in by tall hills that carry unusually tortuous roads, even by New Zealand standards!

The Top of the South possesses a unique sense of place that somehow imparts the laid back and relaxed vibe that the area's locals are renowned for. The landscape may not feature the big-ticket photographic trophies of its southern neighbours, but it has a holistic beauty that captivates visitors and in those moments when light, weather and land coalesce, wonderful photographic opportunities present themselves.

Farmland near Methven, with Mt Hutt in the background. TS

Tussocks near Castle Hill, on the road to Arthur's Pass. ss
OPPOSITE Farmland beneath the Torlesse Range, near Castle Hill. TS

ABOVE AND OPPOSITE Otherworldly limestone formations at
Kura Tawhiti (Castle Hill) Conservation Area. ss

OVERLEAF Farmland near the South Canterbury village of Fairlie. TS

The road to Mesopotamia Station, Rangitata River Valley. TS
OPPOSITE Summer storm clouds brew near Methven. TS

Seal pups play beneath the waterfall at Ohau Creek, north of Kaikoura. SS
OPPOSITE A pair of Dusky dolphins off the Kaikoura coast. TS

Shags (cormorants) bask in the first rays of the day, Kaikoura peninsula. TS
OPPOSITE Dawn light on the Seaward Kaikoura Range. TS
OVERLEAF A three-minute exposure excentuates the visual impact of the
Archway Islands at Wharariki Beach, Golden Bay. SS

ABOVE AND OPPOSITE The windswept sand dunes of Wharariki Beach, Golden Bay. TS
OVERLEAF The Brunner Peninsula spot-lit by early morning light, West Bay,
Lake Rotoiti, Nelson Lakes National Park. TS

THE NORTH

It seems fitting that Cape Reinga, New Zealand's most northwesterly point, should be punctuated with a rather pretty lighthouse – a maritime beacon extending both welcome and warning to the ocean expanse beyond. The sea literally defines the shape of the nation on all of its borders, and the coast is seldom more than an hour or two's drive from even the most inland locations.

Travel north of the Bombay Hills and the relationship between land and sea becomes inescapably intimate. Here, the landmass winnows to a narrow belt of land that features in Maori mythology as the tail of Maui's great fish. New Zealand's largest city, Auckland, sprawls over an isthmus that at one point narrows to little more than 1200 metres wide between the Tasman-fed Manukau Harbour and an arm of the Hauraki Gulf that opens to the Pacific Ocean on the east coast.

Travelling from the dry, cold climes of Central Otago to the balmy, humidity and cultural diversity of subtropical Northland is like arriving in another country for our family. As soon as we get north of Auckland, we tend to cling to the coast and move our campervan from one gorgeous beach to the next. The pace of our lives slows dramatically in the Far North – our most recent trip stretched from 18 days into five weeks of fishing, swimming and relaxing – such is the appeal of the barefooted lifestyle!

It is the coast that draws our attention as photographers also – the thin line between land and sea providing the most compelling opportunities in this final northern stretch of our little island nation.

Cape Reinga Lighthouse at sunset. ss

Looking toward Tapotupotu Bay from the coastal walkway. TS

Coastline near Pataua. TS

Pohutukawa tree in full bloom, Ngunguru, Tutukaka Coast. SS
OPPOSITE Sunrise near Matapouri Bay. TS
OVERLEAF A solitary flax flower, Sandy Bay, Tutukaka Coast. SS

ABOVE AND OPPOSITE Views from the Whale Bay walking track. SS
OVERLEAF Early morning at Paihia Harbour, Bay of Islands. TS

A December afternoon near Coromandel township. SS
OPPOSITE Te Hoho/Sail Rock at sunrise, Cathedral Cove, Coromandel Peninsula. TS
OVERLEAF Mares Leg Cove, Coromandel Peninsula. SS

CENTRAL NORTH ISLAND

The North Island is not overly endowed with real mountains. From a Southerner's perspective, a real mountain towers above its surroundings, sports a snowcap during winter and certainly doesn't have trees covering its summit. Very few mountains meet these (strictly unscientific) criteria north of Cook Strait, but almost all of those that do are spectacular, thanks to the North Island's dominant natural force – volcanism.

The North Island's tallest mountains (Ruapehu, Tongariro, Ngauruhoe and Taranaki) are all active or dormant volcanoes. These shapely mountains are all capable of morphing into fire-breathing, magma-spewing cauldrons at the drop of a geological hat, a fact that Todd can attest to after witnessing the (terrifying) 1995 Mt Ruapehu eruption first-hand from the slopes of Turoa skifield.

These mountain-building volcanic forces are on full display in the central portion of the North Island. This part of the country sits atop the Taupo Volcanic Zone, named for the largest volcano in the system – the one lurking deep below Lake Taupo. The zone stretches northeast from Tongariro National Park's trio of volcanoes toward Taupo and Rotorua before disappearing beneath the Pacific Ocean beyond Whakaari/White Island.

The volcanic plateau is a hugely interesting part of the country to photograph because it is full of extreme contrasts and weird aberrations that are seen nowhere else in New Zealand. Somehow, this compact area manages to incorporate a desert, steaming cliffs, geysers, orange-rimmed hot lakes, boiling mud pools and a volcanic cone so perfect that it appears to be a leftover Hollywood prop.

We photographed many parts of this landscape for the first time as part of this book project. Our time in Tongariro National Park, chasing elusive gaps in Mt Ruapehu's ever-present cloud cap, was the highlight of a month-long photography trip throughout New Zealand. We will be returning soon, now that our eyes have been opened to the photographic possibilities contained within this compact wedge of the New Zealand mainland.

The mineral-encrusted rim of Champagne Pool, Waiotapu geothermal area, Rotorua. ss

Source of the Hamurana Springs, Rotorua. ss
OPPOSITE Cathedral Rocks, Waimangu Volcanic Valley, Rotorua. ss

Inquisitive cattle on farmland beneath Mt Ruapehu, near Tangiwai. ss
OPPOSITE Mt Ruapehu and foothills near Ohakune. ss
OVERLEAF Mt Ngauruhoe viewed at dawn from high on the Tukino skifield road,
with Lake Taupo in the distance. ss

Mts Ngauruhoe and Tongariro from Scoria Flat on the Bruce Road, Whakapapa. SS
OPPOSITE A distinctive cloud cap forms over Mt Ngauruhoe. TS

ABOVE AND OPPOSITE Stunted vegetation in the Rangipo Desert on Mt Ruapehu's eastern lee side. SS

Mahuia Rapids on the Whakapapanui River, Tongariro National Park. TS
OPPOSITE Tawhai Falls, Whakapapa, Tongariro National Park. TS

TARANAKI, HAWKE'S BAY
AND LOWER NORTH ISLAND

The windswept landscape of the lower North Island and Taranaki may be comparatively subdued by New Zealand standards but, nonetheless, this combined area contains many pockets of landscape interest.

The western reaches of both the lower North Island and Taranaki lie open and exposed to the persistently wet and windy weather thrown off by the Tasman Sea. The combination of high rainfall and highly arable pasture has destined the majority of this land to be given over to a variety of agricultural uses.

In the lower north, the plains cede to the Tararua and Ruahine ranges, which form a north–south-oriented spine that demarcates the west and east coast landscapes. These ranges may be relatively low but they nonetheless provide an effective barrier to the Tasman's weather, wringing much of the moisture from westerly weather systems. Over the Tararua and Ruahine ranges, respectively, lie the Wairarapa and Hawke's Bay regions. The dry nor'west winds that carry over the mountains lend both of these landscapes a pleasantly sun-baked appearance during the summer months – these winds also conspire to make the Wairarapa coast one of the windiest places in the country.

For us, the photographic highlight of this part of the country is Mt Taranaki (also known as Mt Egmont). The near-perfect conical form of this dormant volcano sits proud above the surrounding plains and is complemented by beautiful expanses of coastline to the north of New Plymouth. In the lower north, the best photographic opportunities lie along the rugged coastline and in vignettes of the rural landscape. Te Mata Peak, near Havelock North, is a wonderfully craggy aberration in the Hawke's Bay hill country that made our two fleeting visits to that region very worthwhile indeed – we will be passing that way again soon!

Mt Taranaki from the Pouakai Ridge. TS

ABOVE AND OPPOSITE The perfect volcanic cone of Mt Taranaki from Waiiti Beach. SS

Sheep graze in hill country near Lake Ratapiko, Taranaki. ss
OPPOSITE Farmland near Eltham, Taranaki. TS
OVERLEAF Mt Taranaki reflected in an alpine tarn on Pouakai Ridge. ss

ABOVE Looking north toward Napier from Te Mata Peak, Hawke's Bay. TS
OPPOSITE Beach near Waihua, Hawke's Bay. TS
OVERLEAF Sunrise atop Te Mata Peak, Hawke's Bay. TS

Sheep grazing near Masterton. TS

Rangitikei River near Mangaweka. ss
OVERLEAF Dawn at Castlepoint, coastal Wairarapa. ss